STILL STANDING STRONG

Finding My Freedom By Facing My Truth

LaShaunda Johnson

Copyright © 2021 by **LaShaunda Johnson**

All rights reserved. No part of this publication may be reproduced, distributed or transmitted in any form or by any means, including photocopying, recording, or other electronic or mechanical methods, without the prior written permission of the publisher, except in the case of brief quotations embodied in critical reviews and certain other noncommercial uses permitted by copyright law. For permission requests, write to the publisher, addressed "Attention: Permissions Coordinator," at the address below.

LaShaunda Johnson/Rejoice Essential Publishing

PO BOX 512

Effingham, SC 29541

www.republishing.org

Contact author at LJ_ministries@outlook.com

Unless otherwise indicated, scripture is taken from the King James Version.

Scripture quotations marked (NIV) are taken from the Holy Bible, New International Version®, NIV®. Copyright © 1973, 1978, 1984, 2011 by Biblica, Inc.™ Used by permission of Zondervan. All rights reserved worldwide. www.zondervan.comThe "NIV" and "New International Version" are trademarks registered in the United States Patent and Trademark Office by Biblica, Inc.™

Still Standing Strong/LaShaunda Johnson

ISBN-13: 978-1-956775-02-0

LCCN: 2021921078

LaShaunda Johnson had every reason to give up, but she continued to stand strong while trusting in God. Before she was born, the enemy wanted to take her out, but God had a plan. She was abused but overcame it. As she trusted in God, He continued to do the miraculous in her life and favored her. "Still Standing Strong" is a powerful book that will encourage you to endure despite circumstances. You will find inspiration as you read the pages inside. Quitting is not an option. If God blessed LaShaunda Johnson to overcome, He will do the same for you because He is no respecter of a person.

Kimberly Moses
CEO Rejoice Essential Magazine

TABLE OF CONTENTS

ACKNOWLEDGMENTS..vii
INTRODUCTION...1
Chapter 1: Before God Formed Me...................2
Chapter 2: God's Grace and Strength...............6
Chapter 3: God Sent Me An Angel...................9
Chapter 4: Being Present But Not Present.......11
Chapter 5: Dear to My Heart............................13
Chapter 6: Gone But Not Forgotten 15
Chapter 7: My God My Protector....................22
Chapter 8: I Am Fearfully and
 Wonderfully Made.........................26
Chapter 9: I Pressed Through My Pain............31
Chapter 10: Healing/Deliverance Shall Be
 Your Portion..................................35
Chapter 11: God Covered Me 42
Chapter 12: Think It, Speak It, & Watch
 It Manifest......................................44
Chapter 13: God Is A Healer.............................47
Chapter 14: My God My Provider 54
Chapter 15: This Too Shall Pass........................58
Chapter 16: Do You Trust Me?..........................62
Chapter 17: My Journey....................................65

Chapter 18:	The Devil Lost Again	68
Chapter 19:	God Kept Me Again	70
Chapter 20:	My Praise Kept Me	73
Chapter 21:	I'm Still Standing	77
RESOURCES		80
ABOUT THE AUTHOR		81

ACKNOWLEDGMENTS

First, I want to thank God for trusting and allowing me to go through different situations so that I'm now able to tell my story.

Special thanks,

I want to give a special thanks to my husband, Christopher Johnson, my best friend, someone who has never given up on me, drives me to be the best and always pushes me towards my purpose.

INTRODUCTION

Have you ever experienced so much pain that you didn't see any way out? Standing was the last thing you wanted to do, but there was always something that wouldn't let you give up. Even amid depression, neglect, molestation, and illness, there was a grace that covered you. Empowering you to endure the process of becoming who you are. In this book, I am transparent about the traumatic experiences that occurred in my life. But I am equally as open to the manifestations of true healing and deliverance, as well. My condition was not my conclusion; I had an expected end. Instead, every dark situation was an opportunity for God to allow me to experience his light. Through it all, I am because of God's Grace Still Standing Strong.

CHAPTER 1

BEFORE GOD FORMED ME

Jeremiah 1:5 (NIV), "Before I formed you in the womb I knew you, before you were born I set you apart; I appointed you as a prophet to the nations."

It was the Summer of August 1983 in Queens, New York. My mother was 18 years old when she realized that she was pregnant with me. During the time of her pregnancy, my parents were still in high school. As soon as she found out that she was Pregnant, she immediately told my father, who was the only one that knew. So many emotions hit her at once. She had no idea what she was going to do with a child. She wasn't ready to be a mother. She was ashamed and confused. How could she provide for a child when her single mother could barely provide for her and her siblings?

In spite of her struggle, my mother was able to keep the pregnancy a secret for several months. However, as months passed, the truth came out. When my grandmother realized she was pregnant, my mother burst into tears and confessed, "Yes, Mommy, I'm pregnant." Finally, after six months of secrecy, despite being ashamed, she was relieved.

Six months into her pregnancy, abortion wasn't an option. My mother didn't want anyone to know. She chose to keep the pregnancy a secret. She decided to give me up for adoption and began looking into resources for unwed mothers. They eventually located a facility in Brooklyn but told everyone that she went down south to visit family.

My mother lived at the facility for a couple of weeks but was very uncomfortable. The women that lived there were pregnant and homeless. She started thinking and saying to herself, "I don't belong here. I'm pregnant but not homeless." In the back of her mind, she knew she needed to stick to the plan. Even though she hated that place, she stuck to the plan and kept it moving. During her time there, my grandmother would visit her periodically. After nine months had passed, my grandmother strongly suggested that she reconsider keeping it a secret.

Psalms 139:13 (NIV), "For you created my innermost being; you knit me together in my mother's womb."

They decided to keep me and were going to tell the family that Sunday, after church. As my mother began to pack and move back home to Queens, she went into labor. On route to the hospital, my family received the unexpected news of my impending arrival. Excited but surprised at the news, the family patiently awaited my arrival. Now that my mother's family knew and had come together, the isolation of the previous nine months was over. She was now free from her bondage.

Psalms 21:11 (NIV), "Though they plot evil against you and devise wicked schemes, they cannot SUCCEED."

No matter what the enemy tries to plot against your life, always know that God already knew you before He formed you. The enemy might try his best to kill you. However, he can't take what God already placed in you. So what has GOD placed in you? God has placed in us His purpose.

Jeremiah 29:11 (NIV), "For I know the plans I have for you, declares the LORD, plans to prosper you and not to harm you, plans to give you hope and a future."

Even before I got here, the enemy desired to take me out, but God already had a plan for my life and purpose. Proverbs-19:21 (NIV), "Many are the plans in a person's heart, but it is the LORD's PURPOSE that PREVAILS." God revealed His will in me, so I was victorious over the forces that opposed me.

CHAPTER 2

GOD'S GRACE & STRENGTH

Proverbs 31:25 (NIV), "She is clothed with strength, and dignity, she can laugh at the days to come."

The woman possessed with a sober mind, a deep source of strength, and a profound sense of her worth, can face her future with joy. She doesn't have any fear, knowing who she trusts and having done her duty to the utmost of her ability.

On Monday, June 4, 1984, at 9:26 pm, my journey began after nineteen hours in labor. My mother said, "It was love, at first sight, the moment she first laid eyes on me. I was the best thing that had ever happened to her. She would do it all over again because I was worth it." There were no words that could describe the joy she was feeling. She was excited and grateful to have given birth to a girl that looked just like her. All her doubts and fears immediately left. She was reminded of Nehemiah 8:10, "This day is holy to our Lord. Do not grieve, for the joy of the LORD is your strength."

She was no longer worried about the feelings or concerns of others. The only thing that mattered to her at that very moment was her new bundle of joy that she held. She was determined to make it work no matter what she had to do. God graced my mother with strength and dignity! The grace to push through and move on. Women were built to push. We push life out of us. The power of your push gives life. So whatever you do, never stop pushing. There was a strength that made her feel as though she could do anything. She was able to move past the fears that had held her hostage for nine months.

Proverbs 22:6, "Train up a child in the way he should go; and when he is old, he will not depart from it."

I believe that a strong foundation is necessary for healthy growth. So often, we may not understand God's method or ways, but we know that He doesn't make mistakes. For example, when I was younger, God placed my mother's oldest sister, in my life because I would need guidance as a child in my walk of faith. I wasn't aware of why but I am thankful. Her presence, teaching, guidance, and prayers aided me in connecting with God. She knew her assignment, and I appreciated her obedience to the voice of the Lord. Anytime I needed her, she was there.

CHAPTER 3

GOD SENT ME AN ANGEL

In August 1991, a year I would never forget, God sent me an angel, Coye Harris, better known as Jamaal. At the age of 7, I didn't realize he was my saving grace, but God knew just what I needed. Sometimes we don't understand God's plan for our lives, but we must never forget that God has a purpose for all things. At this time in my life, I didn't know he was my Angel and that He was God-sent until I was older. During this time, he and my mother were dating. He would always stop by 207th Street in Queens to visit, and we would play Red Light Green Light, 123, and Mother May I. Those were the good old days. We would be out there for a long time enjoying each other. He never made me feel like I was a burden or an outsider.

Jamaal was the source of so many good things that happened during my childhood. He became to me what my biological father never was - a daddy. He stepped in and took care of me just as if I was his own. No matter how hard times got, he always kept a smile on his face and never complained. He was my father. He symbolizes strength and wisdom and has always been a man with so much humility.

CHAPTER 4

BEING PRESENT BUT NOT PRESENT

Even though I knew my biological father for as long as I could remember, we never connected. It was weird having my father around but not feeling the connection, and I never understood the reason. During his visits, I could always rely on him to bring me new clothes that he made for me. I never saw much of him, but when I did, it was only in passing.

Building a relationship requires spending time with one another. Unfortunately, it wasn't easy to build anything with my father because he was never present. I knew that he loved me, but it was evident that parenting wasn't his top priority. He had other things that were more important to him at that time.

Although everyone told me he was a good person, I never had the opportunity to get to know him for myself.

Now that I'm older, I can see why God blessed me with Jamaal because my biological father wasn't there. God knew that I would need a father in my life for the years to come. The things my biological father didn't do, Jamaal did. I can say that I was Jamaal's little girl from the age of 7 years Old. He took me in and raised me as his own. I was able to experience a father and daughter relationship, and he showed me what a real father truly was to a daughter.

CHAPTER 5

DEAR TO MY HEART

In 1994 my grandmother called to tell us that my biological father had been shot and killed. I was so shocked, hurt, and confused. I couldn't wrap my head around it. I stood there staring at the wall, and I began to cry uncontrollably. My biological father was dead. It was the worst feeling in my life. Even though we never connected, he was still my biological father. Just knowing that he was never coming back made me cry even more. As I sat there on the couch and cried, my mother just held me. That was my first experience with death.

I attended his wake and then his funeral. As I walked down the aisle, I began to cry. I couldn't help but notice that those around me were crying too.

Every time I tried to pull myself together, the realization that my father was gone would hit me again. The feelings were so deep, and my heart was so heavy. For some reason, it was a lot worse than when I received the news that he passed. As I approached the casket, I kissed him for the last time on his forehead and again on his cheek.

I knew that I would never see him again, so I continued to kiss him and tell him how much I loved him. Finally, it hit me that I would never be able to see his eyes again. I cried, not understanding why he had to leave so soon. My emotions were all over the place. The first funeral I ever attended was my father's funeral, — a man who will always be dear to my heart.

CHAPTER 6

GONE BUT NOT FORGOTTEN

Nehemiah 8:10 (NIV), "So don't be sad. The joy of the Lord makes you strong."

September 14, 1995, I was 11 years old when my mother gave birth to my new brother, Najee Kassim Harris. I was so happy and excited for the latest addition to the family. He was the most beautiful baby boy I had ever seen. He was chunky, light-skinned, with a head full of curly jet black hair. He was my baby brother, and I loved him unconditionally. It was a bond that could not be broken. It was a different type of love that I had for him. Everyone loved Najee. He loved the water, and taking baths was one of his favorite things to do. He was the happiest baby with such a beautiful smile. He could look at you and smile, and you would start laughing. He brought so much joy to our family.

In February of 1997, my family visited my Grandmother in North Carolina for a couple of days. My Dad and Najee went to Florida straight from North Carolina to visit his parents. I kissed Najee and told him that I'd see him when he gets back home. He cried because he wanted all of us to go together. My heart was so heavy seeing him cry. I held back my tears because I didn't want to leave him, but I knew he would only be gone for a couple of days. It was the first time that we were ever apart. Even though I wanted to go, I couldn't go because I had school.

I spoke to Najee and my dad every day on the phone while they were visiting Florida. One particular day, I called and asked my dad to pass the phone to Najee. My dad attempted to get Najee by calling him several times but no answer. I remember asking my dad to call him again because I wanted to speak to him, still no answer. Finally, my dad said, "He's in the back playing with the kids." I told my mother that I was going to my best friend's house and I'll call him when I get back. After visiting my friend for a few hours, I decided to head back home.

I walked into the house to my family in my mother's room with a devastated look on their faces. I immediately asked, "What's wrong?" No one said anything, so I knocked on my mother's door. My Uncle answered the door, "Come on, LaShaunda. You're coming to stay with me for a couple of days." What's going on?" I asked. "Your mother has to run to Florida to go get your brother," My Uncle said. I want to go." I yelled. He said. "No, she will be back in a couple of days." I was so confused because I knew something was wrong but couldn't figure it out. Everyone was whispering to keep me from hearing. It made me nervous and scared at the same time.

From that day on, I asked my uncle when they would be back because I missed Najee. I wanted to see him. "Your mother is going to meet Jamaal, and they are coming right back," he replied. She's going there for a few days and will return to New York. It didn't make sense. Why would she pick them up in Florida when the plan had been for us to meet back in NY?

A few days later, my uncle told me my mother and Jamaal were heading back to New York. Later that afternoon, we headed to the airport to meet my family. That couple of days felt like forever, but the time had come. I was excited to see my baby brother.

Words couldn't describe how I felt. I believe I talked about him the entire trip to the airport. We parked the car, went inside, and waited for them. We waited and waited. After waiting for about an hour, I finally saw my parents walking out of the airport. But there was one problem, Najee wasn't with them.

I was 13 years old and desperately needed God like never before. God was my strength at this moment in my life. Never would I have ever thought this would happen so soon.

Immediately, I asked, "Where is Najee?" I can't wait any longer to see him. My mother looked at me with heavy tears in her eyes and with trembling lips, "He's not coming back. He's gone." What do you mean he's not coming back? Where is Najee?" I asked again. She said, "Najee drowned in the pool at Jamaal's parents' house. He's gone." I stared at her in confusion. I couldn't process what she was telling me. I was speechless. I didn't believe her. She continued, "That day you called your brother, he never came to the phone because he drowned." On February 16, 1997, Jamaal's father was cleaning the pool and forgot to lock the gate back. He wasn't expecting them to arrive early. Later that day, Najee was found dead in the pool. The pain I felt was so unreal. I could only imagine what my mother was feeling. The doctors pronounced the death of Najee Kassim Harris on February 16, 1997, at 6:34 pm.

I immediately fell to my knees with tears in my eyes and screamed, "NOOOO. NOOOOOOO, not Najee." I yelled, again and again, "Not my brother!" I cried with disbelief. The news my mother shared was tragic. Najee held a special place in my heart. I protected him, fed him, changed his diapers, took him to the park, dressed him, and taught him how to walk. He was my everything. HE WAS MY BROTHER! I was continuously asking, "WHY? WHY DID HE HAVE TO GO SO SOON? WHY DID YOU TAKE HIM? GOD, WHY?" Back then, people used to say that you weren't supposed to ask God "why," but I didn't care. This day was worse than when my father passed. I was so heartbroken. I felt as though my heart had shattered into pieces that I wasn't able to put back myself. The next several weeks were hard for me. I felt so numb, I cried for days, and every night was a sleepless night. I couldn't bring myself to attend school for weeks.

His death was difficult and he was so young. As tears rolled down my face, my heart was in a knot. The coping of a loss is already hard, but coping with the death of your 1-year-old brother is worse. I prayed to God for strength because I faced a situation where I felt there was no end. My exact words were, "Lord, I need you!" I cried out in desperate need of help. I felt like I was going to lose my mind. I was only 13, but my life had turned upside down and inside out in the blink of an eye. Yet, even in my confusion and hurt, He is still God, and that will never change. Losing my brother by far was one of the hardest things I had to face in life. That experience tested my faith, but God is faithful. We may not understand His ways, but we must trust Him.

Later that week, Najee's body arrived from Florida to the funeral home in Queens. My mother and I went to make final preparations for the funeral. My heart was heavy. The emotions overwhelmed me, and I cried. I tried to be strong for my mother, but I found myself again asking God, "Why?" One of the funeral home assistants approached us and asked if we would like to change his clothing. Finally, my mother couldn't bear the pain any longer, and she left the room. I knew that this would be the last time I would ever see or be able to dress my little brother again. So I muscled up the strength to do what I enjoyed doing when he was alive.

As I laid my head on his chest, my eyes filled with tears. I remember how stiff and cold his body was against my face. I whispered gently, "I will always love you, Najee." I kissed him several times on his cheeks. My heart was full of pain. I rested on his chest, trying to pull myself together, but the tears kept flowing. As I dressed him in his white suit, I noticed how peaceful he looked. He looked like an angel. As I write this, the Scripture comes to mind, 2 Corinthians 5:8, "We are confident, I say, and willing rather to be absent from the body and to be present with the Lord." I hate that I lost my brother so early, but I was confident that he was in a better place.

God was my strength at that very moment. His Word declares in Proverbs 3:5-6 (NIV), "Trust in the LORD with all of your heart. Do not depend on your own understanding. In all your ways remember Him, and He will make your paths smooth and straight."

Najee Kassim Harris, you may be gone but never forgotten.

CHAPTER 7

MY GOD, MY PROTECTOR

Psalms 18:2 (NIV), "The LORD is my rock, my fortress and my deliverer; my God is my rock, in whom I take refuge, my shield and the horn of my salvation, my stronghold.''

Psalms 46:1, "God is our refuge and strength, very present help in trouble."

After Najee's death, I started spending my summers in North Carolina with my Grandmother, my Aunt, or my friend, who I met in the 5th Grade. New York just wasn't the same since the death of my brother. My grandmother was my girl. We just understood each other, and she spoiled me. Her home was my home, but she didn't live alone. At the time, she was in a relationship with a gentleman who was a bit weird. I couldn't make it out, but he was someone I didn't care for at all. I tried to avoid him at every opportunity. My grandmother lived in a two-bedroom home, so the guest room and bath were mine. One night as I was lying in bed, I got this weird feeling that someone was watching me. I looked around to see my grandmother's boyfriend watching me from the bathroom. A few nights later, he came back, but he got into bed with me. I was terrified. I prayed and asked God to protect me. As I began to pray, my grandmother walked in and caught him. Immediately, she made him get out, but that didn't stop him.

He was back in there, night after night, but my grandmother would see him every time and made him leave. I would cry out to God and plea for His protection. I didn't know what else to do. I knew what he was doing was wrong, but I was so timid and afraid I kept my thoughts to myself. I'm thankful that my grandmother would intervene, but mentally, I was terrified and didn't know how to deal with it. All my life, I always kept my thoughts to myself, no matter how I felt. I wasn't very good at handling conflict and confusion. Then, maybe a month later, he was at it again, and it didn't stop. She called his name several times, but he never answered. When she finally found him, he pretended like he was senile. I believe my grandmother didn't trust him. To this day, we've never talked about the situation.

I thank God that she stopped him every time. There is no telling what would have happened. I know that some of you who are reading this are wondering why I never said anything. I was young, and I never had those conversations with my parents about if someone touches you inappropriately what should be done. I'm not saying it can prevent it from happening, but it can reduce the vulnerability to sexual abuse and increases the chances of telling your parents. My grandmother knew, but she thought I was asleep, and she never said anything, so I didn't bother. She loved Him, and I loved her. I had been with her since birth. I loved my mother, but the relationship with my grandmother is solid.

God will protect you when you can't defend yourself. I was afraid, I was timid, I was shy, but I was covered because "Greater is he that is in you than he that is in the world (1 John 4:4)."

My God, who is my protector, my everything, will always be MY ALL AND ALL. God has been that and much more. How do I know? I know because I was born with Christ in me, who is the hope of the glory. A part of me identifies with truth, but I had to come to the knowledge of who I am. In my house, there was no gospel music playing, only when I played it. There was no praying, only when I prayed. So our environment can't alter us if we don't let it.

Even as a child, God always covered and protected me from loss, insult, and injury.

God is my Father and Protector, He is my Shield and the Power that Saved Me.
He is my Place of Safety.
I Call Him (God) Jehovah Sabaoth.
Jehovah Sabaoth-The Lord of Hosts- Means Our Protector "The Existing One" or "Lord.
Jehovah Shalom is who I call on when I need a Peace of Mind, or Peace in general.

CHAPTER 8

I AM FEARFULLY AND WONDERFULLY MADE

Psalms 139:14, "I will praise thee; for I am fearfully and wonderfully made: marvelous are thy works; and that my soul knoweth right well."

God created me in His image and His likeness. I was set apart for such a time as this. Genesis 1:26 says, "And God said, Let us make man in our image, after our likeness: and let them have dominion over the fish of the sea, and over the fowl of the air, and over the cattle, and over all the earth, and over every creeping thing that creepeth upon the earth."

In my younger years, there were times when God would use me to encourage and minister truth to family and friends. When you have been born with a purpose, age doesn't restrict your ability to be used by

God. As long as you are willing and obedient and led by God, all things are possible. I understood then that I had been set apart by God. Even when I felt like I was on the back burner, looked over, or people that I thought were loyal friends walked out of my life. God allowed all those things to happen. There's a season and appointed time for everything and everyone. God has you on reserve as He forms Christ in you. His seal was on me before I entered into this world. God is so faithful and sovereign in all of His ways that He pushed me to be what He called me to be because He watches over His Word.

God told Jeremiah, "You have seen well, for I am {actively} watching over my word to fulfil it (Jeremiah 1:12 AMP)." Because of this calling in my life, I learned that different isn't always a bad thing. It just means you're unique.

One of the gifts that God placed upon me was the ability to see things before they happen. As a child, it was hard to discuss with anyone because my family wasn't spiritual. So, they weren't able to teach me about my spiritual gifts. I could only identify with what God allowed me to experience. So, I relied on God for knowledge and understanding. Occasionally. I would share some of those experiences with family members, but they thought I was crazy. It is impossible to interpret spiritual things without the Holy Spirit.

Exodus 31:3, "I have filled him with the spirit of God in wisdom, in understanding, in knowledge, and in all kinds of craftsmanship." As God revealed things to me through dreams, they were all starting to happen and manifest so fast. My mother called them premonitions.

While "premonition" sounded good, I knew in my heart that revelations weren't premonitions. I was confident that it was GOD revealing things of the Spirit. As I got older, God continued to speak through my dreams, directly to me or through discernment. Listening to gospel music and prayer were the things that kept me connected to God. As the encounters from the spiritual realm increased, I found myself sleeping with a night light and with all of the doors closed for years. God's hands have always been on my life. I had to get to know him. I attended Baptist churches, but they didn't teach on the 5-fold ministry from Ephesians 4:11, "And he gave some, apostles, and some prophets; and some, evangelists; and some, pastors and teachers."

I was only familiar with the office of a pastor. For years, I asked God to connect me with people who understood me and relate to the things I had experienced spiritually. For example, I'm not saying anything is wrong with those who are Baptist. Certain Individuals are Called to different Levels of God's Word. Matthew 13:8, "…but others fell into good ground, and brought forth fruit, some a hundredfold, some sixtyfold, some thirtyfold" (KJV). I was among individuals who didn't speak my language. I knew that God was calling me higher in the understanding of his Word. I wasn't in the right environment, which is essential in our growth process. Can a fish live outside of water? Of course not! I am a spiritual being having a human experience. I come from the Spirit of God. So I desired to be amongst those Spirit-led believers. These teachings of Jesus guided me toward the people that could help me find my way. Matthew 22:14, "For many are called, but few are chosen." John 4:24 states, "God is a spirit: and they that worship him must worship him in spirit and truth."

At that moment, I felt lost because God desired my worship, and I couldn't. King David shared a similar feeling when he writes, Psalms 139:13-14," You alone created my inner being. You knitted me together inside my mother. I will give thanks to you because I have been so amazingly and marvelously made. Your works are miraculous, and my soul is fully aware of this. I will praise Thee; for I am fearfully and wonderfully made: Marvelous are thy works; and that my soul knoweth very well. ''Fearfully, Wonderfully, and Marvelous. You know me as the one who formed me but I cannot begin to comprehend this creature you have fashioned. I can only look upon him with awe the wonder and Praise You.''

CHAPTER 9

I PRESSED THROUGH MY PAIN

Earlier I mentioned I regularly spent my summers in North Carolina. One summer, I decided to stay with my Aunt instead of my grandmother and my best friend,. I didn't feel comfortable staying with my grandmother while her boyfriend was living with her. My best friend and I had known each other for years. They lived in a trailer park five minutes from my aunt's house. It was always a good time when her and I got together. However, one evening, when her and I were asleep, her father would sneak into the room and molest me. I felt so ashamed and disgusted. Night after night, he repeatedly forced himself on me while using his fingers for pleasure.

I was traumatized. I didn't know what to do or what to say. My best friend's father was touching me inappropriately. I was about 12 years old, and my first encounter with a man was with my best friend's father. Some of you may be wondering why I continued to go back. Honestly, I saw them as family. I was ashamed to mention this to anyone, just as I was with my grandmother's boyfriend. Finally, after the third incident, I built up the courage to tell my bestfriend. She responded with a tone as if it wasn't a surprise to her. The conversation didn't go anywhere. A few nights later, I was awakened by her drunk father with his hand pressed in my vaginal area. I tried to get her attention, but he was gone by the time she woke up. I had anger that built up in me towards this man because I felt violated, vulnerable and nasty. I knew then that I could no longer stay there. The next day I went to my aunt's house to tell her about my experience of being molested.

She said, "LaShaunda, stop going over there if he touches you." I looked at her and was blown away by her response. I inhaled deeply as my eyes filled with tears, so I walked away. I was never the type to show my emotions or let anyone know how I felt. I regretted telling her. I wanted to be rescued from my pain and my shame; instead I was rejected. Rejected by those who said they love me. I didn't know what to do. I was already timid, but now I had to deal with victim-blaming.

As if being molested wasn't enough, now it was my fault?! I struggled with trying to feel normal, but I could still smell him on me. I showered at least twice a day, trying to scrub the scent off me. I cried, asking God, why? Why did you allow this to happen to me? I then shifted the anger from her dad and started blaming myself. I hated the situation, I hated him, and I hated myself. I needed help, but I didn't know how to get it. The one time I opened up and expressed my feelings, I got shut down. So I decided to put the situation in the back of my mind and never think about it again. Years later, I realized that I was in bondage. What I thought I conquered was still there and had a significant negative impact on my life.

I was a Girl
A Girl, young and innocent
A Girl, who didn't like confusion
A Girl, who was scared
A Girl, who was confused
A Girl, who cried herself to sleep at night
A Girl, who always had a smile on her face
A Girl, who was very shy
A Girl, who thought it was her fault
A Girl, who loved
I was just a Girl

I was a girl who cried out to God about everything. But that's all I knew how to do was cry out to God, and God kept my mind at peace. God was my comfort.

CHAPTER 10

HEALING AND DELIVERANCE SHALL BE YOUR PORTION

Psalms 9:9 (NIV), "The Lord is a place of safety for those who have been beaten down, He will keep them safe in the times of trouble."

2 Corinthians 10:3-5, "For though we walk in the flesh, we do not war after the flesh: For the weapons of our warfare [are] not carnal, but mighty through God to the pulling down of strongholds; casting down imaginations, and every high thing that exalteth itself against the knowledge of God, and bringing into captivity every thought to the obedience of Christ."

As Christians, while we believe in the Spirit, we don't realize how much of our mind is a battleground.

Jesus teaches in John 8:36 that His truth will set us free from bondage. It was at this point in my life that I fell into a deep depression. I wanted to make it all go away by taking my own life. Everything I experienced was too much to deal with on my own. Life was harder than ever, and I didn't think I could make it. I remember taking pills several times, but the last time was worse than most. My heart began to flutter, and I became dizzy and light-headed and vomiting. Finally, I cried out to God and asked him to take the feeling away. I made this vow several times to the Lord, but I meant it this time. I promised if he takes this desire away, I will never do it again.

Everywhere I turned, there was one obstacle after another. I couldn't get a break. I knew that God's Word tells us not to lean on our understanding, but nothing made sense. Life seemed to get the best of me. The more I cried out to the Lord, the more He helped me.

He was my comforter who regulated my mind to press forward. God was my reason for living and not giving up. He kept me even during my darkest hours. God helped me to stand when no one else could. I always felt Him, even from a little girl. It was something on the inside that just wanted to say, "Thank you, Lord." If I couldn't speak, I would wave my hands. I knew He was right there. There was always something that made me want to praise Him despite what I was going through. God was always there to see me through.

"Even in the storm, at the darkest moment of your life when you are hanging by a thread, HE IS GOD; You cannot be lost because you are held in the palm of his hand. If I'm going through a storm that means there is always a way for me to come out."

It was the darkest hour in my life, and God was my light, the light that shines in the darkest place. "For His word declares in Psalms 27:1 (NIV), "The LORD is My Light and my Salvation whom shall I fear? The LORD is the stronghold of my life of whom shall I be afraid?" He is my God. God continued to find me during the darkest places in my life. God is the creator, mighty and strong. He is my keeper, my mind regulator, my, all in all, my God the faithful One, the Lord God almighty, my Lord, my provider, my healer, the Most High God, the Lord my master, the Lord my Shepherd, the Lord my banner, the everlasting God. With my pillow wet with tears, I felt a peace that overshadowed me. God came to see about me like He always does. His presence covered me. It was a peace that covered me, for His Word declares that "He is Our Peace (Ephesians 2:14)." God is Jehovah

Shalom. When I didn't want to get out of bed, locking myself in my house for days because of the pain, God helped me get up and stand even when I didn't want to. He helped me push through my pain. He is Omnipotent. He has Unlimited Power.

God Didn't Keep You Alive Without a Purpose

Everything that I Experienced-GOD DID IT-GOD ALLOWED IT TO HAPPEN

"I declare and decree that I have free passage for my prayers to ascend into the realm of the supernatural and will not be earthbound." I declare that the anointing of God has loosed every chain and broken every yoke of bondage in Jesus' name. I pull down every mental stronghold with prophetic authority. "I signal the Archangels Michael and Gabriel to reinforce me as I advance into new levels, new dimensions, new realms, and territories in Jesus' name." I declare and decree that angels are working on your behalf. I tap into the prophetic vein by the anointing of God. "I decree and declare that the fire of the Holy Ghost will dismantle the works of darkness." I send the fire of the Holy Spirit to the North, East, South, and the West. I come against every spirit of witchcraft, and the prince over every region, I close every open demonic portal in Jesus' name. Anything that is not of God, I command it to die right now. God, we praise and worship you. You are Our Father our God, You are Jehovah Gibbor, the Lord mighty in battle. Lord, we thank you in advance for fighting our battles.

Psalms 24:7-10, "Lift up your Heads, O ye gates; and be ye lifted up, ye everlasting doors; and the King of glory shall come in. "Who is this King of Glory? The Lord strong and mighty, The Lord mighty in battle. Lift up your heads, O ye gates; Even lift them up, ye everlasting doors; And the King of glory shall come in. Who is this King of glory? The LORD of hosts, he is the King of glory. Selah." (KJV)

As Rebecca Greenwood writes about the strongholds that bind us she says, "We have all experienced battles with thoughts that need to be diffused and defeated. We all battled the mental strongholds, though we may not have realized it. A stronghold of the mind is a lie that Satan has established in our thinking that we count as true but is actually a false belief. We need to embrace these lies, they affect our attitudes, emotions, and behaviors."

The Apostle Paul writes in Romans 8:5-8, "For those who live according to the flesh set their minds on the things of the flesh, but those who live according to the spirit set their minds on the things of the spirit. For to set the mind on the flesh is death, but to set the mind on the spirit life and peace. For the mind that is set on the flesh is hostile to God, for it does not submit to God's law; indeed, it cannot. Those in the flesh cannot please God. You, however, are not in the flesh but in the spirit, if in fact the spirit of God dwells in you. Anyone who does not have the spirit of Christ does not belong to him. But if Christ is in you, although the body is dead because of sin, the Spirit is Life because of righteousness.''

Once you can express what you have been through in your life is the first step to breaking the stronghold that enslaves your mind once you open your mouth and realize you tell your mind what to do. Then, you begin to let go of your past and realize that your past is not your fault. Only in the name of Jesus can the chains of bondage be broken.

I decree and declare over the one reading this that your life will change in the name of Jesus. You will experience healing and deliverance in your life in the name of Jesus. The fire of the Holy Ghost shall break every curse, stronghold, and word of the enemy. The Lord shall be your strength during whatever you're going through. I declare that your past will no longer hold you in captivity. I silence the echoes of the past in the name of Jesus. I come against every tormenting spirit and send the fire of the Holy Ghost to the nations.

I come against every unseen force of darkness and every foul-smelling spirit. I come against the prince of the power of the air that the blood of Jesus shall dismantle it. I decree and declare that whatever you are going through shall be lifted off you as you continue reading this book. Jehovah Rapha is healing. Jehovah Mephalti is delivering in the name of Jesus. I believe that healing/deliverance is taking place at this very moment. I pray that you feel the tangible love of Jesus.

CHAPTER 11

GOD COVERED ME

Isaiah 53:5 (NIV), "But He was pierced for our transgressions, he was crushed for our iniquities; the punishment that brought us peace was on him, and by his wounds we are healed"

When I was in high school, there was a guy I dated for a couple of years. Everything a girl desired in a relationship, we had it. I was captivated by his charisma, his smile, and his sense of humor. After dating for about three years, I knew I wanted to share that moment every girl looks forward to; I wanted him to be my first. I decided to be intimate with this guy because I was in love with him. Months later, I told my mother that I was sexually active. Surprisingly, her response wasn't horrifying. However, she made me schedule an appointment to see an OBGYN. I arrived home from school one day, and I received a phone call from my doctor with some devastating news.

She informed me that I tested positive for a sexually transmitted disease. I felt like my heart was literally on the floor. No one ever took the time out to educate me about protecting myself from any sexually transmitted diseases. I didn't understand the severity of my condition, but my doctor explained that it was still treatable. I was stunned. It was my first time having sex. Once my mother came home, I told her what the doctor told me. Without reservation, we went for treatment at the Clinic. My mother was so calm and understanding, so I wasn't worried about the news I received. She explained to me the importance of protecting myself from unprotected sex. Through it all, God covered me.

CHAPTER 12

THINK IT, SPEAK IT, WATCH IT MANIFEST

John 14:14, "If Ye Shall Ask anything in my name, I will do it."

It was the summer of 2002, and I was so excited to finish high school. I couldn't wait to visit my family in North Carolina. I had plans to celebrate not only my graduation, but I was 18, officially an adult. After being in North Carolina for a couple of days, I started working at Wendy's full time and started saving. North Carolina had begun to feel like home, so I started making living arrangements. I knew the cost of living in North Carolina compared to New York was a lot cheaper.

My Grandmother drove me around to look for places for rent. There was one in particular that I loved. The blinds were open, so I looked through the windows, and it was empty. I turned to my Grandma and said, "This is mine right here. I claim it, and God is going to give it to me. I walked around the house, and I had some oil in my purse that I prayed over. I laid my hands on the doors, windows and claimed it.

My grandmother took me to the office around the corner to speak to the landlord. I gave her the address that I was interested in, and she told me that one wasn't available. The new resident would move in within two weeks. It was then that I remembered the scripture in Hebrews 11:1, "Now faith is the substance of things hoped for, the evidence of things not seen." I put my faith to work, knowing that God was going to do it. I told the landlord I still wanted to apply for that address that I saw, and I trusted God. I knew in my heart that God was going to make a way no matter what. I began to thank God in advance for making a way out of no way.

This was the first time I trusted God for something that I wanted – like this house. Of course, I trusted God for other things, but this time it was a little different. So I figured it was worth a try.

A couple of days later, the landlord called. She said, "I don't know how this happened, but the lady that was supposed to move in had a family emergency. She's not able to move. So if you still want it, it's yours." I told her, "God did It." I prayed, and God gave it to me. I was 18 and finally moved into a place of my own, and I loved it.

No matter what obstacles we face, if God spoke it, then it shall come to pass.

CHAPTER 13

GOD IS A HEALER

Mark 5:34, "And he said unto her, Daughter, thy faith hath made thee whole; go in peace, and be whole of thy plague."

I had recently turned 23 years old. My mother was planning a surprise birthday celebration for my father in New York. I decided to leave North Carolina early to help her out. It was the beginning of summer, and the weather was beautiful. As soon as I arrived, we went shopping for the party. While walking down the stairs, a sharp pain hit me in the lower part of my stomach. I knelt with one hand on my stomach and the other hand on my knee. The pain was so intense I couldn't describe it – a sharp stabbing pain. I was on fire. My mother, on the other side of the store, didn't see me. I didn't want her to worry, so I didn't say anything. But the pain would come and go.

As we started to leave, the pain returned. It was so bad; I couldn't walk. My mother ran over to me, "What's wrong? Are you ok?" Uncontrollable tears rolled down my face, "No, I'm in a lot of pain." She asked me to describe it. I gave her the details. She said, "I had felt similar pain when I had a tubal pregnancy." Her and another man helped me upstairs. It felt like I was never going to make it because the pain was so intense. Finally, a couple of minutes later, the pain stopped. Days went by, and I was pain-free. I made it to the surprise birthday party for my dad.

After we got home, I laid on the bed, and the pain came back. However, this time it was unbearable, and I couldn't move. I curled up in a fetal position and sobbed. I went from laying on the bed to rolling on my stomach to leaning over the bed on my knees, anything to get some relief. The only thing I could do was cry.

I knew it wasn't normal because I had never felt this type of pain before. I was in my old room in the basement. I yelled out to my mother for help. She immediately came to see about me, but I wasn't able to move. As soon as the pain stopped, my parents took me to the hospital that night. Suddenly, while we were in the car, the pain started again. By this time, a lot of people were waiting, so the wait time was extremely long. I knew they had to go to work in the morning, so I told them that I would wait. My mother made me promise to go to the clinic in the morning before my flight back to North Carolina.

I got up the next morning and went to the clinic. The doctor ran several tests and said that it looked as though I was having a miscarriage or an Ectopic Pregnancy. The only thing they knew for sure was that my pregnancy test was positive. The doctors told me I needed to get to the hospital. During the ambulance ride, I called my mother to let her know what was going on. I could hear the nervousness in her voice. She told me not to let the doctor do anything until she arrived.

During the ride, there were so many thoughts going through my mind. I was nervous and scared, it was my first time in an ambulance, and I was alone. I just found out that I was pregnant. I wasn't sure what was wrong with the baby. I never even knew that I was pregnant. When I arrived at the hospital, they rushed me straight to the ultrasound room from the ambulance. The nurse mentioned that I was a little over six weeks pregnant and the baby was located in my tube. She showed me the baby on the screen. That was the third time I heard about a pregnancy in my tube (Ectopic Pregnancy), but I still didn't know what that meant. As soon as I left the ultrasound room, they rolled me on the bed to the hallway, where my mother waited to see me. I was so nervous about the news that I had just received. My mother was there with several family members. My mother, Aunt, and one of my cousins did everything they could to assure me that everything would be ok because they too had experienced an Ectopic pregnancy and a couple of others in the family. I remember my mother saying, "This will be the best sleep of your life," as she started to chuckle.

Everything just happened so fast. I didn't have time to think. I needed to have emergency surgery, and it couldn't wait another minute. ''The Doctor stated that The Ectopic Pregnancy almost killed me. I looked at the doctor and said, "My God is a Healer, and the Devil is a liar."

When I woke up from surgery, a lot of my family was there. I was in so much pain in my stomach area. The doctor said, "The tube was damaged, and they couldn't save it. I still had another tube, so getting pregnant wasn't ruled out completely.

I was in the hospital for seven days. It was hard for me to use the restroom, bathe or walk because of my restrictions after surgery. I laid in bed. Days of being on a liquid diet made me weak, and I had no strength. My mother and the nurse had to help me with everything, from bathing, walking, etc. When my doctor came to visit me, I asked if I could have anything other than liquid. He responded, "Unfortunately, not at the moment. He needed to monitor me very closely." I had been so close to death. Tired, frustrated, and hungry, I had no choice but to tough it out. That whole experience was overwhelming, and I just wanted it to be over.

> During my hospital stay, I prayed this prayer -
> God is Jehovah Rapha, the One Who Heals.
> Not just your body, but your mind and your heart.
> Jehovah Rapha is who I call on when I need healing.

A year after the Ectopic pregnancy, I started feeling sick. For nearly a month, I couldn't keep anything down. I was dizzy and nauseous. I thought maybe it would pass, but it didn't. Finally, after two weeks without a bowel movement, I knew something wasn't right. I went to the nearest clinic, and they thought it was constipation. I tried medication after medication, but nothing worked. It had been well over 30 days since I had a bowel movement. I couldn't eat anything, and the doctors were clueless. The only thing I knew would work, and that was prayer. So I went to the bathroom and closed the door, and I began to pray.

I commanded every infirmity to die as I laid hands on my body and decreed that it should line up with the Word of God. I called on Jehovah Rapha, the God that heals. I determined in my prayer that everything out of order shall line up. When I go back to the doctor, they will find the reason behind this illness. I did not doubt that he was with me, for we call him Emmanuel, "God is with us (Matthew 1:23)." Sometimes we have to remind ourselves that He's there and He will never leave us nor forsake us (Matthew 28:20). Moments after I finished praying, my ex-boyfriend took me back to the same hospital, but it was a different doctor. After he ran a few tests and completed an X-ray, he immediately saw the issue. The tissue from the Ectopic surgery hadn't healed correctly, which caused my bowels to back up. I needed emergency surgery right away. I called my mother to inform her of the surgery, she asked that they wait for the surgery until she arrived, but I decided to proceed with the surgery.

The doctor said, "I'm sorry, we can only wait until the morning for her to get here." Later that night, they tried to run a few other tests. As the nurse attempted to insert tubes into my stomach several times through my nose, I couldn't take it; it was too painful. The nurse finally gave up after seeing the anxiety on my face.

The next morning, as they prepared me for surgery, fear started to hit me. Psalms 27:1 states, "The LORD is my light and my salvation; whom shall I fear? The Lord is the defense of my life; Whom shall I dread?" (KJV) Before this, I had never seen inside of the operating room. It was cold with big equipment everywhere. There was a group of doctors and nurses waiting to operate on me. At the time, all I wanted was my mother by my side. She was still traveling to get there. They placed the oxygen mask on my face with anesthesia with no warning. I instantly started choking. I tried to raise my hand to get their attention to remove the mask, but no response. I wanted to remove it myself, but it was too late; the anesthesia had already started working. Hours later, I woke up in the recovery room to see my nurse there. She said my family had arrived. I could barely talk because of the tubes that were down my nose and throat. Sometimes God allows sickness in your life to prove that he truly is - Jehovah Rapha.

CHAPTER 14

MY GOD, MY PROVIDER

Philippians 4:9 (NKJV), "The things which you learned and received and heard and saw in me, these do, and the God of peace will be with you."

I was finally able to return home from surgery. The doctor gave me specific instructions to refrain from working for approximately two months. I knew that I couldn't afford to do that financially because I lived alone. My bills were behind; car payment was $1,000 past due, no money for groceries, car insurance delinquent, etc. Every day I was on edge about my car, praying and hoping they wouldn't repossess it. Finally, I decided to call the finance company and explain my situation and they agreed to work with me. That was a relief because I had no idea how I was going to bring my account current. It was a trying time in my life, but I didn't allow the devil to shake my faith. God had already proven to me that He was my way maker.

One day I received a notification to go to the Leasing Office where I was living. I went there, and the landlord handed me an envelope with a check inside. "What's this for?" I asked. He said, "Only certain individuals qualified, and you were one of them." I had never applied for any assistance. God is faithful. Jehovah Jireh (Genesis 22:14) provided right when I needed Him. The check was the exact amount of my light bill. I received that check for months. After months of being off of work, I was finally able to return. I knew it would be hard playing catch up, but I would do what I could and trust God for the rest.

After about a year, I wanted to live somewhere else. I was tired of staying in the projects. There was a small 2nd-floor apartment in another house across from my aunt's house. I reached out to some men from the church I was attending to help me move. As we began to move, I realized the space was too small, and nothing would fit. I was frustrated and didn't know what to do. I had ended my current lease, but now the new place wasn't sufficient enough. While the landlord understood and refunded my money, I was homeless again.

During this search for another house, my aunt agreed to let me stay with her. But, unfortunately, many nights after working an 8-hour shift and a 45-minute commute, I would find a locked door and no one home. So I had to stay over with friends or sometimes at a motel.

I started staying with a close friend around the winter season. She had recently moved into a slightly older but sturdy house. She was generous enough to allow me to stay with her and her son. Unfortunately, there was no central heat or air. The only source of heat was kerosene heaters and miniature plug-in heaters. I began to pray and asked God for strength because this was the second time I found myself homeless. I was faithful in my giving and paying my tithes, but it was difficult to trust God as I laid on an air mattress freezing, wrapped in layers of clothing. Four months later, she moved to the apartment complex I had just left.

I felt like my life was going backward. I ended up back where I started. Often, I would say, "I can't wait to get my own place." My friend redirected my words and told me not to say: "I can't wait. But "I'm ready to move." There is power in our words. We have to speak those things that aren't as though they are. "I can't wait" is not faith activated. "I am ready" are words of faith. It releases His Word from Heaven.

From that day on, I confessed every day to the Lord that I was ready to move. What I confessed for months was now my reality. I moved into my place again. God provided.

CHAPTER 15

THIS TOO SHALL PASS

Things were starting to fall in place for me; life was better. I graduated high school, moved to North Carolina, got a new job, and moved into my first apartment. However, months after my relocation, I started to miss home. In my heart, I knew I was where God wanted me, but I really missed my friends and family. I was depressed and lonely. Sometimes God has to remove us from our comfort zone and set us apart while he works on our character. We have to be broken so that Christ can live.

I tried to pray, but I couldn't find the words to say. I could only dwell on my depression and loneliness. Many times I thought about moving back, especially when I couldn't participate in family gatherings or reunions. Traveling there wasn't an option. My income at the time was only sufficient to cover my overhead. There would be days when I didn't want to be bothered. I would lock myself in the house and cry. It was really becoming a war within myself. Everything that I'd been through, every thought that I had suppressed, every bad experience that caused me to shut people out, had me feeling lost and confused. I had experienced so much at an early age and not knowing how to deal with it. I felt there was no one in whom I could confide in. Choosing not to deal with negative emotions or ignoring feelings is unhealthy. We have to acknowledge what's in us because it will eventually leak out in some way or another at some point in life. Trying to press toward the mark in life with dead weight can be exhausting, but I'm reminded of a scripture, Psalms 55:22, "Cast thy burden upon the Lord, and he shall sustain thee: he shall never suffer the righteous to be moved."

I truly felt like I was on an island all alone. It was nothing anyone had done to me. I needed to be in a place where I could consecrate myself and allow God to heal me internally; no longer could I live in denial. So I laid before the Lord and asked Him to renew my mind. Purge me from every hurt, violation, and pain that kept me from walking into my purpose. For me to seek His kingdom first, I had to set aside every weight. God was molding me into the woman He created me to be. Whatever you may be going through, I prophesy to you that your life will never be the same, but this too shall pass. It's our faith that grants us access to Him.

Activate your faith because, without it, it is impossible to please him. Anytime you may feel defeated, muscle up some praise and worship. Create an environment for God to reside and manifest. Jesus tells us in John 4:24, "God is a spirit: and they that worship him must worship him in spirit in truth." God is seeking true worshippers. Where is your worship? Where are the TRUE Worshippers? Not just when He answers prayers but at all times. God is looking for those that don't mind worshiping Him for who He is and not for what He can do. Where are the ones that will stand bold and say not my will but Your will, whatever you need me to do, I will do it, tell me where to go, and I'll go, Lord, you can use me. I said that to say this, don't be His part-time lover, but love Him at all times. Through the good and bad because it's all working for your good.

It was in the most challenging times in my life when God taught me what to do; He taught me how to pray, how to shift the atmosphere, and taught me how to praise through His Word. The Bible teaches us in James 5:16, "The effectual fervent prayer of the righteous avails much." Prayer is essential in our walk of faith. The Bible tells us that we should always pray (1 Thessalonians 5:17). Prayer is what keeps us conscious of God. That's why it must be a continual thing. We have to train our minds to pray at all times. Remember, it is our faith that grants us access to the Father. Live by faith, believe by faith, and pray by faith. There is power in your tongue.

Whatever your process may be, ask God for the grace to endure it. Even Jesus prayed this way in Luke 22:42,. "Father, if it is your will, take this cup {Of Suffering} away from me. However, your will must be done, not mine (God's Word Translation)."

I realized that every test I went through was preparing me for a testimony. We have to pass the test to have a testimony as Revelation 12:11 teaches us, "And they overcame him by the blood of the Lamb, and by the word of their testimony; and they loved not their lives unto death." The testimony is not for us, but it's for the people to encourage them that God is faithful and His word is true. I am a living testimony that I know God is who He says He is.

CHAPTER 16

DO YOU TRUST ME

Romans 8:28, "And we know that for those who love God all things work together for good to them that love God, to them who are called according to his purpose."

Sometimes in life, we allow what we go through to keep us from trusting God because it may not feel good. I will admit that trusting God is not something you learn overnight. Jesus learned obedience through the things He suffered. So it's a process. The more we connect with God and continue to build a relationship, trusting Him becomes less of a struggle. Financially, I was struggling to maintain. The bills were coming in faster than the money. During my time at Direct TV, I was blessed to have two beautiful friends who became my spiritual sisters in the Lord.

We had each other's back. Proverbs 27:9, "Perfume and incense bring joy to the heart, and the pleasantness of a friend springs from their heartfelt advice." We prayed together, cried together, laughed together, and encouraged one another. It was about a week before Memorial Day. I was at the end of my rope. There were some things I needed God to do for me. As I was traveling on the road, praying and crying. I heard the Lord say. "Do you trust me?" I said, "Yes Lord, I trust you. He responded again. "Do you really trust me?" Yes, Lord. I trust you. When I arrived at my apartment complex, I saw the landlord. The Lord instructed me to say, "Hello and asked him if he had something for me?" So I obeyed God. The landlord responded, "Yes, I do, actually."

He handed me an envelope. I needed to move into a 1-bedroom apartment to finish the renovations on all the two-bedroom apartments. I didn't understand what the Lord was doing. I knew I was just tired of moving, tired of praying, tired of praising, and tired of struggling. I was tired of everything altogether. But giving up wasn't an option. I had to stand on His Word.

God is all-knowing. Nothing is ever a surprise to Him. Even when you feel as though you don't know the Way, Jesus tells us, "He is the Way" (John 14:6). After waiting a long time for God to speak, He finally provided specific instructions for me to follow. I didn't grow weary in my faith because I knew God would direct my path if I acknowledged Him. God was very strategic with what he wanted me to do. If we ever find ourselves lost in life, it's because His Spirit is not leading us. I then knew what to do, expect, and next steps to take. I allowed my situation to be in control instead of my God. I could have asked for assistance from family or friends, but I knew that God was building my faith in Him, especially since He asked me if I trusted Him. God had already planned my next moves. Psalms 37:23, "The steps of a good man are ordered by the LORD: and He delighteth in His way."

CHAPTER 17

MY JOURNEY

Growing up, I always felt like an outcast. It didn't matter if it was my family or friends. It was always a struggle to fit in. I had a hard time trusting people because of past experiences. Those I did trust and were loyal to either walked out of my life or let me down. For example, I had a best friend of 20 years. We grew up together, and we were more like sisters, but she walked out of my life, no explanation. I tried to contact her, but no response. I was hurt and didn't understand why my best friend of 20 years didn't feel like she could talk to me about whatever it was that was bothering her.

It's weird that you can be with people and feel as if they can't see you. People always thought I was moody or mean, but it wasn't that. I had built a wall to protect myself from being hurt again. I wouldn't let anyone get close to me or my heart. I later learned that my insecurities and hurt caused me to feel like an overlooked outcast. I didn't know who I was. I had to find myself and who God called me to be. The enemy uses our hurt to make you feel like the victim, but the enemy can't do anything that God doesn't allow. He is the prince of the power of the air, but I have dominion over him. He desires to make us feel unloved. We have to shut the door and silence the Father of Lies. Love is in us because God is in us. Oprah Winfrey once said, "Life is the journey of learning to love yourself first and then extending that love to others in every encounter."

Searching for the woman inside of me wasn't easy. She was always there, but I had to let the little girl go to move into what was to come. The Apostle Paul teaches us in 2 Corinthians 5:17: "Therefore, if anyone is in Christ, he is a new creation, old things have passed away; behold, all things have become new." I couldn't embrace the new until I was delivered from reliving my past. My past was hindering me from moving forward because I carried my childhood trauma into my adult life. It kept me from tapping into my true potential.

I knew the potential was there but had no idea or guidance on how to navigate through the hurt and brokenness. My mother always had an open-door policy, but I understood that she was dealing with a life of her own. Losing her child really took a toll on her. I thank God for her; she has been a blessing and I love her dearly. I was born on purpose for a specific purpose. I didn't come from my mother; I came through my mother. God used my mother as a gateway to bring me here on earth. I learned through other more seasoned women that God allowed me to encounter. That broken little girl was still there, crying out for help. God had to heal me from the inside out. Learn to trust the journey, even when you don't understand it.

Jehovah Mephalti- (The Lord Our Deliverer)

Psalms 18:2 (NIV), "The LORD is My Rock and my Fortress and my Deliverer. My God, My Strength, in whom I will Trust; My Shield and the horn of my Salvation, my stronghold.''

CHAPTER 18

THE DEVIL LOST AGAIN

Mark 10:45, "For even the son of man did not come to be served, but to serve and to give his life a ransom for many."

I look at my situations now and say that I didn't go through them for myself. God allowed me to go through them so I could witness the goodness and faithfulness of God. We have to realize that we must experience the darkness to appreciate the light. I came here to be a servant to God's people. Every hurt, disappointment, every setback, every illness, and every let down; God allowed it. My past prepared me for where I am today. I can stand in confidence that it was because of His grace, mercy, and strength that I survived every trial.

The devil thought he had me, but he lost the battle again. The Bible teaches us in Deuteronomy 20:4, "For the Lord your God is the one who goes with you, to fight for you against your enemies, to save you." God fights our battles. No devil will ever take me out of my place in Him. I realize the power that lies in my tongue. I have the authority to shift the atmosphere. God Uses us in this realm to manifest His word. I can command healing over my body. Now that I know who I am, I know for a fact that I am a threat to the devil's territories. That is why the devil tries so hard to prevent us from knowing our true identity in Christ. He tries to steer us from our purpose and make us feel that we are not loved. Never allow the enemy to make you feel like God doesn't love you. The Bible teaches us in 1 John 4:19, "We love him, because he first loved us." The enemy will plant seeds in our minds, and if we dwell on it long enough, we will start to believe it. We must dismiss anything contrary to God's Word. If you don't, a STRONGHOLD will form.

No matter what we go through, God will take our mess and turn it into a message. So don't let what you've been through or what you're going through stop you from moving forward. God will turn your test into a testimony, but you must first pass the test. If God did it for me, He would do it for you, and this too shall pass.

CHAPTER 19

GOD KEPT ME AGAIN

I was scheduled to work the 11 pm-7 am shift at the nursing home. That 10:00 pm alarm wasn't all that welcome. My best friend was living with me, and she had already left for the night. However, this night was tough because I was exhausted from working overtime. I had to go in because I knew that I couldn't afford not to. After my shift was over, I went home, and the police surrounded my apartment. It was completely blocked off. An officer and the landlord met me at the front door. The officer told me they needed to get into my apartment because of a shootout the night before. A man had been shot and killed right in front of my apartment. The evidence they needed was inside, and they needed my permission to enter. I granted the officers permission. I was grateful because there could have been a different outcome.

There were bullets everywhere. I thank God that He got me up to go to work. I would not have been here to tell my story today. Even when I was living in the world, I never forgot where my help came from, and God kept me (Psalm 121:2). When there is a purpose for your life, grace will cover you.

** The enemy might try to detour or distract you from your Purpose. Whatever God placed in you, no one can ever take that from You. **

I tried to do things my way for years but it didn't work. My ways are not His ways

**Just because you can't see it doesn't mean that you are going the wrong way. **

**Just because it doesn't make sense at the moment doesn't mean it's wrong. **

**A lot of things that the Lord does doesn't make sense to the natural eye, you have to see it in the Spirit. **

It doesn't make sense to us – Which Is the Natural Man but it makes sense to your Spirit but the spirit knoweth all.

It will start to make sense by and by.

CHAPTER 20

MY PRAISE KEPT ME

Psalms 9:1 (NKJV), "I will praise you, O Lord, with my whole heart; I will tell of all Your marvelous works."

Praise is the most powerful tool you could ever use. It causes things to change. True praise isn't just from our mouth, but it comes from the heart. It was my praise that brought me through the hard times in life. The times when I felt like I couldn't make it. As I matured in God, my perspective on suffering changed. I no longer viewed it as "a bad thing" but as an opportunity for God to prove his sovereignty. For if we suffer with Christ, we shall reign with him also (2 Timothy 2:11). My suffering pushed my praise; praise that taught me to honor God, praise that brought deliverance, praise that knocked down walls of resistance, praise that preceded blessings, and praise that fueled joy which gave me strength. God was working on my behalf and behind the scenes. I realized that it wasn't about me but Him and His glory. If we ever feel alone, remember that he inhabits the praises of his people, He lives in our praise (Psalm 22:3).

My mind shifted from the Church-to-Kingdom. We were always taught in the church to give God thanks after he gives us something. However, in the kingdom, we are taught to give God thanks first. So I start giving God thanks in advance for what He's already accomplished. I don't wait for God to do it.

When I was going through depression because of issues in my life, I started to command my mind to get in line. I knew that God would fight all of my battles. I began to exalt and glorify the Lord because everything He does is right and all of his ways are just, the devil thought he had me, but he lost again.

I gave God a Todah Praise. When I open my mouth and say "Lord, I Thank You, Lord, I Love You, Lord, you are Amazing, Thank You Lord for Keeping My Mind, Lord, I thank you for who you are, Lord, you are Awesome, you are Sovereign in all your ways, there is none like you, Higher Lifted up are you.

When my body was afflicted with pain, I started to come against infirmities that tried to attach itself to me and command healing, and I called Him Jehovah Rapha because that's who He Is. I began to give God Yada Praise. I would wave my hands and command healing. When I realized that my bills were due and I didn't know how they would be paid, I shouted with the voice of triumph. I began to give God a "Hallelujah Praise," which is the highest praise. As I began to praise Him, unexpected checks came in the mail. I also gave God Tehillah Praise by singing praises to Him. I tapped into God's Kingdom (Hebrews 4:16).

We have to learn how to create an atmosphere, an atmosphere of praise. We have to build a relationship with God. I realized that if I just offer up praise and acknowledge Him in all of my ways, not some of my ways, He will direct my path (Proverbs 3:5-6). I realized that my life is not mine, but it belongs to the Lord.

There was one morning around 5:15 am I was on my way to work. I started listening to my gospel music. I felt the need to pray against car accidents. I began to declare in the atmosphere. I had just got off the highway, stopped at the stop sign and an 18 wheeler appeared and was a couple of Inches from knocking my car straight off the road. The devil tried to take me out that morning but I deposited a praise in the atmosphere, something shifted. I had to say "Lord, I thank You." See that's what PRAISE will do!

During my younger years, there were times that I was homeless or had to rent a house. God's Word came forth through prophecy that God was going to give my husband and I a house. In 2021 we were approved for our first house, that we built from the ground up, Prophecy fulfilled! God did just what He said He was going to do. If God spoke it, it shall come to pass. We stood on His Word for over 5 Years, in spite of how it looked. In spite of our circumstances, we put a praise on it and the prophecy manifested. We are now walking into MANIFESTATION.

CHAPTER 21

I'M STILL STANDING

Jeremiah 29:11(NKJV), "For I know the thoughts that I think toward you, says the Lord, thoughts of peace and not of evil, to give you a future and a hope."

If I'm going through a stormy season in my life, there is always a way out. God has already created a way of escape because there is an expected end.

-When I thought I was going to lose my mind, God regulated it.
-When I was hungry, God fed me.
-When I was homeless, God provided.
-When my bills were due, He made a way.
-When I was molested, God healed and delivered
-When my heart was broken, God restored it.
-When I felt like I was by myself, His word declares Deuteronomy 31:6 (NIV), "Be strong and cou-

rageous do not be afraid or terrified of them, for it is the LORD your God who Goes with you: He will never leave you nor forsake you.''

-When I Felt Like I Lost My Way, His Word Declares John 14:6 (NIV), "I AM the way the truth and the Life, No One Comes to the Father except through me.''

-When my body was afflicted with pain and sickness, God proved Himself to be Jehovah Rapha
-How do you stand when you feel like you're about to lose your mind? You stand on His Word-
-How do you stand in the midst of a storm? You trust God-
-How do you stand when you feel like ALL HELL is breaking loose in your life? You trust God-

How do you stand when you feel like you've been in the fire? You trust God. Even though you've been through the fire, you won't smell like smoke when you come out. However, it is a consuming fire destroying demons, healing sickness, shifting the atmosphere of obedience in your life.

I'm still standing by the grace of God. Even through my mess, He still loves me. God doesn't see us where we are but where He called us to be. When

he sees me, he sees the sacrifice of His Son. And if the Son is in the Father and that Father is in the Son, He is in me. Your condition is not your conclusion. God loves each of us. God is concerned about our purpose. That's why He watches over His Word because it can't, and it won't return unto Him void (Isaiah 55:11). I am standing, and you will continue to stand by His grace because His grace is sufficient, and He will get the glory.

I can say that I am still standing because God wonderfully created me in His image. I'm grateful for who I am because God pushed me to be the woman I am today. I'm still standing because of His grace. I can walk in my purpose knowing who I am and what God has called me to do. As a girl, I was violated, homeless, looked over, timid, confused, lost, broken, and lacking confidence, but by His grace, I can say that I am a woman of God; Prophetess LaShaunda Johnson.

RESOURCES

Crisis Call Center
1 (800) 273-8255 Text: "ANSWER" to 839863
http://crisiscallcenter.org/crisisservices-html/

Suicide Prevention
1 (800) 273-8255
https://suicidepreventionlifeline.org/

Crisis Text Line
text HOME to 741-741
https://www.crisistextline.org/
HYPERLINK: "https://www.crisistextline.org/"

Depression Hotline
(many resources phone numbers)
https://www.psychguides.com/guides/depression-hotline/

ABOUT THE AUTHOR

    LaShaunda Johnson was born in New York City in 1984. She's the daughter of Pearl and Coye Harris. LaShaunda graduated from Beach Channel High School in June 2002. Later in life, she decided to pursue a career as a professional hairstylist, which led her to receive her Cosmetology License in 2018 from Corinth Academy of Cosmetology. God called LaShaunda over 37 years ago to be a Prophetess to the nations. She was raised under an Apostolic Ministry, where she served under the leadership of her spiritual father, Apostle Curtis Lake III. LaShaunda faced many obstacles in her life that pushed her to develop a strong relationship with God. Through her trials, her faith was tested, but she never wavered. She stood against all odds because she realized that greater was coming. She strives to encourage others that God is a man of His word. She is determined to mentor, train, and develop the Sons of God to come into the knowledge of who they are and fulfill their purpose through the Spirit of Love, and the Spirit of Truth.

INDEX

1

123, 9

5

5-fold ministry, 28

A

ability, 6, 26, 27
abortion, 3
account, 54
acknowledge, 59, 75
adult, 44, 66
afraid, 23, 24, 37, 78
age, 9, 12, 26, 59
air, 26, 41, 56, 66
air mattress, 56
airport, 17, 18

Amazing, 74
ambulance ride, 49
anesthesia, 53
angel, 9, 21
anointing, 38
anxiety, 53
apartment, 55, 56, 58, 63, 70
Apostle Paul, 39, 66
apostles, 28
appointed time, 27
Archangels, 38
ashamed, 2, 3, 31, 32
assignment, 8
atmosphere, 60, 69, 75, 76, 78
attitudes, 39
August, 2, 9
aunt, 31, 32, 55, 56
Aunt, 22, 31, 50
authority, 38, 69
Awesome, 74

B

baby, 15, 17, 49
back burner, 27
Baptist churches, 28
basement, 48
bathroom, 23, 52
battleground, 35

battles, 39, 69, 74
beautiful, 15, 47, 62
bed, 23, 38, 48, 50
behaviors, 39
best friend, 16, 31, 32, 65, 70
Bible, 60, 69
bills, 54, 62, 75, 77
birthday, 47, 48
blessings, 73
blood, 41, 61
body, 20, 21, 40, 51, 52, 69, 75, 78
bold, 60
bondage, 4, 33, 36, 38, 40
bowel movement, 51
boy, 15
boyfriend, 23, 31, 32, 52
broken, 15, 38, 40, 58, 67, 77, 79
Brooklyn, 3
brother, 15, 17, 18, 19, 20, 21, 22
burden, 9, 59

C

captivity, 35, 40
car, 18, 48, 54, 75, 76
car insurance, 54
carnal, 35
casket, 14
cattle, 26

chain, 38
charisma, 42
cheaper, 44
check, 55
cheek, 14
chest, 20, 21
child, 2, 7, 8, 25, 27
childhood, 10, 66
choking, 53
Christ, 24, 27, 35, 40, 58, 66, 69, 73
Christians, 35
chuckle, 50
church, 4, 55, 74
Clinic, 43
clothes, 11
clueless, 51
cold, 20, 53
comfort, 34, 58
command, 39, 69, 74, 75
complained, 10
comprehend, 30
confessed, 3, 57
confidence, 68, 79
confident, 21, 28
confused, 2, 13, 17, 33, 59, 79
confusion, 18, 20, 23, 33
conquered, 33
consecrate, 59
constipation, 51

couch, 13
courage, 32
Coye Harris, 9
craftsmanship, 28
crazy, 27
creature, 30
Crisis Call Center, 80
Crisis Text Line, 80
cry, 13, 16, 23, 34, 48, 59
curse, 40

D

daddy, 10
darkness, 38, 41, 68
dating, 9, 42
daughter, 12
dead, 13, 18, 40, 59
death, 13, 19, 22, 40, 51, 61, 66
defeated, 39, 60
deliverance, 1, 40, 41, 73
delivered, 66, 77
deliverer, 22
demonic portal, 38
demons, 78
denial, 59
depressed, 58
depression, 1, 36, 58, 74, 80
Depression Hotline, 80

desperate, 20
detour, 71
devil, 54, 69, 74, 76
dignity, 6, 7
dimensions, 38
Direct TV, 62
disappointment, 68
disbelief, 19
discernment, 28
disgusted, 31
dismantle, 38, 41
distract, 71
dizzy, 36, 51
doctor, 43, 49, 50, 51, 52, 54
dominion, 26, 66
doubts, 7
dreams, 28
drowned, 18
drunk, 32
duty, 6

E

earth, 26, 67
East, 38
Ectopic Pregnancy, 49, 50
educate, 43
emergency surgery, 50, 52
Emmanuel, 52

emotions, 2, 14, 20, 32, 39, 59
encounters, 28
encourage, 26, 61
enemy, 4, 5, 40, 66, 69, 71
environment, 24, 29, 60
escape, 77
evangelists, 28
evil, 4, 77
excited, 7, 15, 17, 44
expected end, 1, 77
eyes, 6, 14, 18, 19, 20, 32

F

face, 6, 10, 19, 20, 33, 46, 48, 53
faith, 8, 20, 45, 47, 55, 56, 60, 61, 64
faithful, 20, 27, 37, 55, 56, 61
family, 3, 4, 15, 16, 17, 26, 27, 32, 44, 45, 50, 53, 58, 64, 65
father, 2, 10, 11, 12, 13, 14, 18, 19, 31, 32, 47
fear, 6, 37, 53
feelings, 7, 14, 33, 59
fetal position, 48
finance company, 54
fire, 38, 40, 41, 47, 78
fish, 26, 29
flesh, 35, 39, 40
Florida, 16, 17, 20
flutter, 36

forehead, 14
forgotten, 21
fortress, 22
Fortress, 67
foundation, 7
fruit, 29
frustrated, 51, 55
funeral, 13, 14, 20
future, 5, 6, 77

G

gate, 18
gifts, 27
girl, 7, 12, 22, 34, 36, 42, 66, 67, 79
glory, 24, 39, 74, 79
God, 1, 2, 4, 5, 6, 7, 8, 9, 12, 18, 19, 20, 21, 22, 23, 24, 25, 26, 27, 28, 29, 33, 34, 35, 36, 37, 38, 39, 40, 42, 43, 45, 46, 47, 50, 51, 52, 53, 54, 55, 56, 57, 58, 59, 60, 61, 62, 63, 64, 66, 67, 68, 69, 70, 71, 73, 74, 75, 76, 77, 78, 79
goodness, 68
gospel music, 24, 28, 75
grace, 1, 7, 9, 61, 68, 71, 79
grandmother, 3, 13, 22, 23, 24, 31, 32, 45
grieve, 7
groceries, 54
growth, 7, 29
guidance, 8

guy, 42

H

hair, 15
happy, 15
harm, 5
hated, 3, 33
heal, 59, 67
heart, 5, 14, 16, 19, 20, 21, 28, 36, 43, 45, 51, 58, 63, 66, 73, 77
heartbroken, 19
Heaven, 56
heavy, 14, 16, 18, 20
high school, 2, 42, 44, 58
highway, 75
holy, 7
Holy Spirit, 28, 38
home, 4, 16, 20, 22, 23, 43, 44, 48, 54, 56, 58, 70
homeless, 3, 55, 56, 76, 77, 79
hope, 5, 24, 77
hospital, 4, 48, 49, 50, 51, 52
hostage, 7
hostile, 40
hours, 6, 16, 36
house, 16, 17, 18, 24, 31, 32, 38, 45, 55, 56, 59, 76
humility, 10
humor, 42
hundredfold, 29

hungry, 51, 77
hurt, 13, 20, 59, 65, 66, 68

I

illness, 1, 52, 68
imaginations, 35
impact, 33
impossible, 60
incense, 63
income, 58
iniquities, 42
injury, 25
innocent, 33
insecurities, 66
insult, 25
intimate, 42
island, 59
isolation, 4

J

Jamaal, 9, 10, 12, 17, 18
Jehovah Gibbor, 39
Jehovah Jireh, 55
Jehovah Mephalti, 41, 67
Jehovah Rapha, 41, 51, 52, 53, 75, 78
Jehovah Sabaoth, 25
Jehovah Shalom, 25

Jeremiah, 2, 4, 27, 77
Jesus, 29, 36, 38, 40, 41, 60, 61, 62, 63
journey, 6, 66, 67, 75
joy, 6, 7, 15, 16, 63, 74

K

kerosene heaters, 56
kids, 16
kill, 4
King David, 29
kingdom, 59, 74
kiss, 14
kissed, 14, 16, 20
knee, 47
knot, 19
knowledge, 24, 27, 28, 35

L

labor, 4, 6
landlord, 45, 55, 63, 70
LaShaunda, 17, 32, 79
laughing, 16
lease, 55
Leasing Office, 55
levels, 38
light, 1, 15, 28, 36, 37, 53, 55, 68
lonely, 58

LORD, 4, 5, 7, 21, 22, 37, 39, 53, 64, 67, 78
loss, 19, 25
love, 6, 15, 20, 32, 41, 42, 60, 62, 66, 69
lover, 60
loyal, 27, 65

M

MANIFESTATION, 76
medication, 51
Memorial Day, 63
message, 69
mighty, 35, 37, 39
mind, 3, 6, 20, 21, 33, 34, 35, 36, 37, 39, 40, 49, 51, 59, 60, 74, 77, 78
minister, 26
miscarriage, 49
molest, 31
molestation, 1
Monday, 6
money, 54, 55, 62
months, 3, 4, 7, 54, 55, 56, 57, 58
moody, 65
motel, 56
mother, 2, 3, 4, 6, 7, 9, 13, 15, 16, 17, 18, 19, 20, 24, 28, 29, 42, 43, 47, 48, 49, 50, 51, 52, 53, 66, 67
Mother May I, 9
mouth, 40, 73, 74

N

Najee, 15, 16, 17, 18, 19, 20, 21, 22
Najee Kassim Harris, 15, 19, 21
nasty, 32
nations, 2, 41
natural eye, 71
neglect, 1
Nehemiah, 7, 15
nervous, 17, 49, 50
new creation, 66
New York, 2, 17, 22, 44, 47
news, 4, 14, 19, 43, 50
North, 16, 22, 31, 38, 44, 47, 49, 58
North Carolina, 16, 22, 31, 44, 47, 49, 58
nose, 52, 53
numb, 19
nurse, 49, 51, 52, 53

O

obedience, 8, 35, 62, 78
obeyed, 63
OBGYN, 42
obstacle, 36
officer, 70
old, 2, 7, 9, 15, 18, 19, 32, 47, 48, 66
Omnipotent, 38
opportunity, 1, 12, 23, 73

opposed, 5
Oprah Winfrey, 66
overnight, 62
overwhelmed, 20
oxygen mask, 53

P

pain, 1, 18, 20, 32, 38, 47, 48, 50, 59, 75, 78
pastors, 28
peace, 34, 37, 40, 42, 47, 54, 77
Perfume, 63
permission, 70
phone, 16, 18, 43, 80
pillow, 37
pills, 36
plague, 47
plan, 3, 5, 9, 17
pleasure, 31
power, 7, 41, 56, 61, 66, 69
praise, 26, 29, 37, 39, 60, 73, 74, 75, 76
prayer, 28, 51, 52, 60
prayers, 8, 38, 60
pregnancy, 2, 3, 48, 49, 50, 51
pregnant, 2, 3, 49, 50
premonitions, 28
presence, 8, 37
prince, 38, 41, 66
prophecy, 76

prophet, 2
Prophetess, 79
prophetic vein, 38
prophets, 28
prosper, 4
protect, 23, 24, 65
punishment, 42
Purge, 59

Q

Queens, 2, 4, 9, 20

R

ransom, 68
Red Light Green Light, 9
refuge, 22
region, 38
regretted, 32
rejected, 32
relationship, 11, 12, 22, 24, 42, 62, 75
relief, 48, 54
rent, 44, 76
resistance, 73
restrict, 26
restroom, 50
reunions, 58
righteousness, 40

road, 63, 76
rock, 22
rope, 63

S

sacrifice, 79
sad, 15
safety, 35
salvation, 22, 53
Satan, 39
scared, 17, 33, 49
scent, 33
schemes, 4
screamed, 19
season, 27, 56, 77
secrecy, 3
seeds, 69
senile, 23
September, 15
servant, 68
sex, 43
sexual abuse, 24
sexually transmitted disease, 43
shame, 32
Shepherd, 37
shield, 22
shocked, 13
shootout, 70

shot, 13, 70
siblings, 2
sickness, 53, 78
sister, 7
sisters, 65
sixtyfold, 29
sleepless, 19
smile, 10, 15, 16, 33, 42
sobbed, 48
soul, 26, 29, 30
South, 38
sovereign, 27
sovereignty, 73
speechless, 18
Spirit-led believers, 29
spiritual realm, 28
spiritual sisters, 62
spoiled, 22
stairs, 47
stiff, 20
stomach, 47, 48, 50, 52
store, 47
storm, 37, 78
strength, 6, 7, 10, 18, 19, 20, 21, 22, 40, 51, 56, 68, 74
stronghold, 22, 37, 38, 39, 40, 67
struggle, 3, 62, 65
SUCCEED, 4
suffered, 62
Suicide Prevention, 80

summer, 31, 44, 47
Summer, 2
Sunday, 4
suppressed, 59
surprise, 32, 47, 48, 63
survived, 68
sustain, 59

T

talk, 53, 65
teach, 27, 28
teachers, 28
teaching, 8
tears, 3, 16, 18, 19, 20, 21, 32, 37, 48
terrified, 23, 78
territories, 38, 69
testimony, 61, 69
thankful, 8, 23
thirtyfold, 29
timid, 23, 24, 32, 79
tongue, 61, 69
tragic, 19
trailer park, 31
transgressions, 42
transparent, 1
traumatic, 1
traumatized, 31
trial, 68

triumph, 75
trouble, 22, 35
trust, 20, 23, 55, 56, 63, 65, 67, 78
truth, 3, 24, 26, 29, 36, 60, 78

U

Uncle, 17
unique, 27
unprotected sex, 43
unreal, 18

V

vaginal area, 32
victim-blaming, 32
victorious, 5
violated, 32, 79
vow, 36
vulnerability, 24

W

war, 35, 59
weapons, 35
weary, 64
weather, 47
weight, 59
weird, 11, 23, 65

Wendy's, 44
West, 38
wicked, 4
windows, 45
wisdom, 10, 28
witchcraft, 38
womanhood, 66
womb, 2, 4
women, 3, 67
world, 24, 27, 71
worship, 29, 39, 60
wounds, 42

Y

yoke, 38
young, 19, 24, 33

www.ingramcontent.com/pod-product-compliance
Lightning Source LLC
Chambersburg PA
CBHW071501070526
44578CB00001B/407